IMAGES
of America

CANASTOTA
AND CHITTENANGO
TWO HISTORIC CANAL TOWNS

HOIST BRIDGE ON ERIE CANAL, BY MOONLIGHT,
CANASTOTA, N. Y.

THE HOIST BRIDGE OVER THE ERIE CANAL BY MOONLIGHT, CANASTOTA. (Courtesy Barbara H. Richardson.)

IMAGES
of America

CANASTOTA
AND CHITTENANGO
TWO HISTORIC CANAL TOWNS

Lionel D. Wyld

ARCADIA

Published by Arcadia Publishing,
an imprint of Tempus Publishing, Inc.
2 Cumberland Street
Charleston, SC 29401

Printed in Great Britain.

Library of Congress Catalog Card Number: 98-88064

For all general information contact Arcadia Publishing at:
Telephone 843-853-2070
Fax 843-853-0044
E-Mail arcadia@charleston.net

For customer service and orders:
Toll-Free 1-888-313-BOOK

Visit us on the internet at http://www.arcadiaimages.com

BY THE SAME AUTHOR

Low Bridge! Folklore and the Erie Canal
Boaters and Broomsticks. Tales & Historical Lore of the Erie Canal
Walter D. Edmonds, Storyteller
The Navy in Newport
The Grand Canal. New York's First Thruway (co-author, Eric Brunger)

Cover Image: A detail of the painting *Lumber Boats at Chittenango* by Robert E. Hager, depicting a scene on the Erie Canal, *c.* 1907. (Courtesy of the artist.)

CONTENTS

INTRODUCTION

Canastota and Chittenango share a growth spawned by the building of the Erie Canal, which opened in 1825 joining Buffalo on Lake Erie with Albany, the state capital, and the Hudson River. The canal provided an artificial inland waterway—the longest continuous canal in the world—across upstate New York. Canastota became an overnight "canal town," situated on the Erie's original route. Chittenango, while not directly on the waterway, became a virtual canal town also, as canal boats for the Erie were built and repaired on the canal just a short distance north, where the Chittenango Canal Boat Landing featured a three-bay dry dock. Just a few miles apart and a short distance east of Syracuse, roughly the half-way point across upstate New York, both villages today have canal-related museums and parks, and are joined by New York State Routes 5 and 13.

They also share much in addition to their canal-related background, for both have a history of early settlement and town folk who were or became leaders in manufacturing, agriculture, industry, and public service. In a more popular realm, Chittenango boasts a unique annual Oz festival each May honoring native writer L. Frank Baum, author of *The Wonderful Wizard of Oz* and other books; Canastota is also home to the International Boxing Hall of Fame, founded there in 1984. Both villages are close to Interstate 90, the Gov. Thomas E. Dewey New York State Thruway. Canastota's Boxing Hall of Fame has an annual Induction Weekend in June, with a Breakfast of Champions, collectors card show, parade, golf tournament, and the induction ceremony. A few miles away, in July, the Chittenango Landing Canal Boat Museum Canal Fest features craft shows, horse-drawn wagon rides, blacksmithing, tinsmithing, stonecutting, and other events.

Canastota and Chittenango: Two Historic Canal Towns offers an insight into two upstate communities that will provide readers with a rewarding look at an important region of eastern America. The history and development of Chittenango and Canastota represent in many ways that of many other villages and towns whose growth—and often their very origins—were linked to the famous Erie Canal, once hailed as "the eighth wonder of the world," and to the transportation revolution and westward movement it brought about.

One
ALONG THE ERIE CANAL

The Erie Canal belongs as much to folklore as to history. Opened in 1825, the Erie was the longest continuous artificial inland waterway in the world, hailed as an engineering accomplishment of unprecedented proportions. It drew visitors from far and near, home and abroad. Historically, the Erie opened the American Midwest to settlement, and served as a commercial waterway transporting farm goods and other freight from the Great Lakes ports and towns across the state. In folklore it was referred to as "The Roaring Giddap" and "The Horse Ocean"—the "eighth wonder of the world," memorialized in song and story.

For the villages of Canastota and Chittenango, the canal brought prosperity, growth, and expansion. The Erie passed just north of Chittenango village, and Chittenango Landing provided an important dry-dock complex for building and repairing boats. In Canastota, thanks to a hometown canal surveyor-engineer, the canal went right through town. In both villages, the Erie Canal created a need for inns, hotels, and restaurants; marine and associated businesses grew up; and area farms and factories found an easy and inexpensive way to ship their goods to markets further along the canal or beyond, connecting to Hudson River boats bound for downriver cities and the metropolis of Manhattan.

THE DRY DOCKS AT CHITTENANGO LANDING IN ITS HEYDAY. This is now a National and State Historic Site, with work underway to restore the area—which includes the sole remaining dry docks of the days of the Erie Canal as an educational and historical center. (Chittenango Landing Canal Boat Museum.)

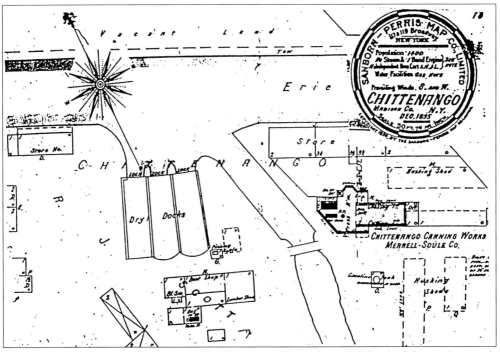

AN INSURANCE COMPANY MAP OF 1895. The map outlines the canal dry dock bays, along with the Chittenango Canning Works, husking sheds, and other facilities at Chittenango Landing. (Chittenango Landing Canal Boat Museum.)

A 96-FOOT CANAL BOAT. It was built at Chittenango Landing boatyards in less than a month. (Chittenango Landing Canal Boat Museum.)

THE CANAL BOAT OSWEGO DOCKED AT CHITTENANGO LANDING. (Chittenango Landing Canal Boat Museum.)

THE CANAL BOAT *SATIE HUGHES* OUT OF FORT HUNTER. (Laws collection, Chittenango Landing Canal Boat Museum.)

ADELBERT, GEORGE, AND THEODORE LAWS. Here they change the towing animals in a typical scene in the Chittenango-Canastota area, as elsewhere along the Erie. A horse that has finished his trick crosses over the "hoss bridge" for stabling onboard the canal boat, as two fresh animals wait on the towpath. (Laws collection, Chittenango Landing Canal Boat Museum.)

A Chittenango Landing Canal Boat Museum card. It shows a scene of the original landing and an old photograph of boaters onboard a working canal boat on the Erie.

THE I.J. NORTHRUP STORE AT CHITTENANGO LANDING. It sold "groceries and provisions" for the boaters working the Erie Canal. (Chittenango Landing Canal Boat Museum.)

ALONG THE ERIE CANAL AT CANASTOTA, A FEW MILES EAST OF CHITTENANGO LANDING. (Chittenango Landing Canal Boat Museum.)

AN ELEVATED LOADING RAMP ON THE ERIE CANAL, CANASTOTA. This view captures a train (background) crossing the canal on a railroad bridge. (Laws collection, Chittenango Landing Canal Boat Museum.)

ALONG THE ERIE CANAL. This scene shows the *Ben F. Wolcott* and other boats tied up near the Canastota grain elevators. (Laws collection, Chittenango Landing Canal Boat Museum.)

Break time. Boaters pose for a picture during a break in the canallers' workday. (Laws collection, Chittenango Landing Canal Boat Museum.)

Erie Canal
Canastota, N.Y

Two boats alongside the berm at a bend in the canal, Canastota. (Laws collection, Chittenango Landing Canal Boat Museum.)

BEFORE THE AUTOMOBILE. Horse-drawn buggies were a frequent sight along the Erie Canal in Canastota. This village, like Chittenango a few miles west, was home to considerable businesses spawned by the canal's opening. The Erie also created numerous jobs related to carriage and wagon manufacture, and fostered western migration as New England Yankees, and some Yorkers as well, were prompted by incentives like the Homestead Act to follow the canal westward to the Ohio country and beyond.

Erie Canal, looking East from Main Street, Canastota, N.Y.

THE ERIE CANAL, LOOKING EAST FROM MAIN STREET, CANASTOTA. (Courtesy Barbara H. Richardson.)

MORE OF THE CANAL AS IT PASSES THROUGH CANASTOTA VILLAGE. (Laws collection, Chittenango Landing Canal Boat Museum.)

THE WIDE WATERS TURNAROUND ON THE CANAL BETWEEN PETERBORO AND MAIN STREETS, LOOKING EAST FROM THE MAIN STREET BRIDGE IN THE EARLY 1900s. The Peterboro lift bridge across the Erie Canal can be seen in the distance. The present-day Canastota Canal Town Museum is located a few doors west of the site of that bridge (since replaced). (Canastota Canal Town Museum.)

A POSTCARD VIEW OF A BRIDGE OVER THE CANAL, CANASTOTA. (Laws collection, Chittenango Landing Canal Boat Museum.)

Erie Canal looking East from Peterboro Street.   CANASTOTA, N.Y.

ANOTHER POSTCARD VIEW. It shows the Canastota Celery Co. building on the right along the Erie Canal. (Laws collection, Chittenango Landing Canal Boat Museum.)

A POSTCARD VIEW OF NORTH CANAL STREET ALONG THE CANAL, C. 1912. (Canastota Canal Town Museum.)

REFLECTIONS IN THE CANAL. They highlight this scene along North Canal Street. (Canastota Canal Town Corporation.)

WINTER ALONG CANAL STREET LOOKING EAST TOWARD OLD HIGH BRIDGE. (Canastota Canal Town Corporation.)

A WINTER SCENE IN 1903. Skaters took advantage of the frozen canal in the winter months. Part of the Parker Provisions canal grocery appears on the left, and the Main Street bridge can be seen in the distance. (Canastota Canal Town Corporation.)

THE OLD CITY HALL. This view, looking across the canal, shows the Canastota Celery Co. (right) and the old city hall. (Canastota Canal Town Museum.)

A TWO-HORSE TEAM. The animals are hitched to an enclosed vehicle along the canal. (Laws collection, Chittenango Landing Canal Boat Museum.)

A TEAM WITH A WAGON. The wagon is loaded with construction girders. (Laws collection, Chittenango Landing Canal Boat Museum.)

CANASTOTA LIFT BRIDGE CONSTRUCTION, 1905. Standing on the scow, far left, is Bert Halsey of Chittenango. His boat, a laker, can be seen at the dock in the distance. (Canastota Canal Town Museum.)

anastola

A PRE-1910 POSTCARD OF CANASTOTA. It provides an especially fine contemporary view of the lift bridge across the Erie Canal. (Courtesy Barbara H. Richardson.)

A CLOSER VIEW OF THE LIFT BRIDGE, PETERBORO STREET, CANASTOTA. (Laws collection, Chittenango Landing Canal Boat Museum.)

A POSTCARD VIEW OF THE BRIDGE LOOKING NORTH, PROBABLY ABOUT 1920. It shows the stairs on each side connecting with village sidewalks. (Canastota Canal Town Museum.)

ANOTHER POSTCARD VIEW OF THE PETERBORO STREET HOIST OR LIFT BRIDGE. (Courtesy Barbara H. Richardson.)

A CLOSE-UP VIEW OF THE BRIDGE STAIRWAY. This picture was reproduced from an original, contemporary sepia-tone photograph in the Canastota Canal Town Museum.

THE LIFT BRIDGE OR HOIST BRIDGE (AS IT WAS ALSO CALLED), MARCH 1925. In the next year or two, with the original canal no longer in use, this famous landmark over the old Erie Canal would be torn down and replaced by a regular village street bridge. (Canastota Canal Town Museum.)

STEREOPTICON VIEW. It shows the Peterboro bridge after the close of the original Erie Canal in the village. (Canastota Canal Town Museum.)

TEARING DOWN THE LIFT BRIDGE ACROSS THE CANAL ON PETERBORO STREET, 1926 OR 1927. (Canastota Canal Town Museum.)

PICNIC ON A CANAL BOAT, 1905. Those were the days! (Canastota Canal Town Museum.)

Two

CANASTOTA:
PEOPLE AND PLACES

Canastota, with its many businesses and diverse industry base, saw an enviable growth in real estate, with many of the residences of manorial proportions. The fact that the state's Grand Erie Canal went directly through the middle of the village assured it more than a modicum of economic success, as it drew with it an associated mercantile trade, restaurants, and shops along the banks and nearby village streets; but, in addition to the blacksmith shops, brick yards, sawmills, feed stores, and taverns spawned by the canal, there were private residences, churches, and schools to keep pace with a growing community.

With the modernization of the canal into the New York State Barge Canal System around 1915 and its course shifted outside the village, the Canastota Canal Town Museum continues to reflect the golden days. Housed in a building built in the earlier canal's heyday along the banks of the original Erie, which formed a veritable "main street" through town, the Canal Town Museum is filled with authentic memorabilia and exhibits.

Canastota today also recalls its connection with the sport of boxing. The International Boxing Hall of Fame chronicles a century of boxing history, including Canastota's own champions, Carmen Balisio and Billy Backus; and each year in June Induction Weekend offers boxing fans an opportunity to meet some of the boxing world's great figures. For more on this, see chapter seven.

A FLOAT FEATURING NATIVE AMERICANS. The sign shown on the float indicates that the village name was derived from the Oneida words "kniste" (meaning *water*) and "stota" (*quiet or still*). The Oneidas referred to the area as a "cluster of pines near still waters." (Canastota Canal Town Museum.)

CAPTAIN REUBEN PERKINS, CANASTOTA FOUNDER. He came to the region along the Seneca Trail in 1807, following the Native-American trails and waterways that later enabled settlers to go westward by cart and stagecoach. Perkins, with a contingent of Oneidas, established ownership of 328 acres of land, the Native Americans receiving a fair share in the transaction. On July 27, 1810, Gov. Daniel D. Tompkins transferred to Perkins letters patent under state law, making him owner of the area. Eventually disposing of his holdings, Perkins sold 100 acres in 1814 and the remaining two-thirds for $8,000 seven years later. Canastota was incorporated as a village on July 27, 1835. (Photograph from a postcard, courtesy Richard Sullivan, Historian, Village of Chittenango.)

NATHAN ROBERTS. He was a teacher of mathematics in Whitestown (later Whitesboro) when, in 1816, Benjamin Wright, who was in charge of the middle section of the planned Erie Canal, appointed him assistant engineer to survey the route from Rome to the Seneca River. Roberts was 40 at the time. He and his wife moved to Canastota in 1817 after he began his work on the canal. (Portrait by William Henry Dorance in the New York State Museum; reproduced with permission from the cover of *Nathan Roberts: Erie Canal Engineer* by Dorris Moore Lawson, courtesy of North Country Books, Inc., Utica, New York.)

THE NATHAN ROBERTS HOUSE IN CANASTOTA, C. 1896. It was located on the old Seneca Turnpike, now New York State Route 5. (Reproduced with permission from *Nathan Roberts: Erie Canal Engineer* by Dorris Moore Lawson, courtesy of North Country Books, Inc., Utica, New York.)

Courtesy of Mrs. Barbara Bartlett

MILTON DeLANO. Influential in Canastota for more than half a century, DeLano served as clerk of the old Town of Lenox and was twice elected sheriff of Madison County. He served in the United States Congress 1888–92. He founded the State Bank of Canastota and was active in starting the Canastota Public Library. (*Canastota Centennial Official Souvenir Program*, July 24–30, 1960; courtesy Rose Raffa.)

CANASTOTA PUBLIC LIBRARY IN 1910 (POSTCARD). A small one-room public library opened in the village in 1896. Philanthropist Andrew Carnegie donated $10,000 to the library and the village provided the lot. The cornerstone was laid in December 1902 and the building was completed in 1905. (Canastota Canal Town Museum.)

A RAILROAD CROSSING, 1920. The first railroad passing through Canastota in 1839 joined the cities of Syracuse and Utica. As Canastota continued to grow as a farming and industrial area, residents felt it might become a major railroad center in the state. While the early railroad line became part of the growing New York Central Railroad system, a Cazenovia-Canastota line was completed in 1870. When the southern route proved successful, it was extended to DeRuyter within two years and then to Cortland and Elmira on New York's southern tier. The line—the Elmira, Cortland and Northern Railroad—later became part of the Lehigh Valley Railroad Corporation. The photograph above, taken February 25, 1920, shows the railroad crossing at Peterboro Street in the village. In 1964 an overpass was constructed, and now Amtrak passengers probably hardly notice the village as they pass overhead. (Photograph by F.J. Walter, courtesy Canastota Canal Town Museum.)

CANASTOTA AS A TRAIN CENTER. In an article in 1885 encouraging businesses to locate in Canastota, the thriving village was said to have the New York Central and Hudson River Railroad, as well as the "terminus of the U.I. & E. Railroad, Erie Canal and the N.Y.W.S. & B. Railroad, all within a radius of 40 rods." (Canastota Canal Town Museum.)

BOOSTING A NEW RAILROAD IN 1893. A movement to establish a Canastota, Morrisville, and Southern Railroad failed, despite the fanfare and the time and effort put into building the makeshift engine and cars shown in this scene. (*Official Commemorative Book—1985*; courtesy Rose Raffa.)

A POSTCARD SHOWING THE CANASTOTA RAILROAD STATION. (Canastota Canal Town Museum.)

THIRD RAIL CARS AT THE STATION IN CANASTOTA (POSTCARD). Further improved modern transportation came with the electrified third rail of the Oneida Railway Co. (Chittenango Village Historian.)

The Weaver, Canastota, N.Y.

THE WEAVER HOTEL, CANASTOTA, IN MODEL-T DAYS. "The Weaver Was First-Class Hotel" ran the caption for this picture postcard of the hotel reproduced in the *Official Commemorative Book* for the village's 175th birthday celebration. A disastrous fire in 1873 leveled a previous hotel at the site, along with 19 other structures in the square bordered by Depot, Peterboro, and Center Streets. (Chittenango Landing Canal Boat Museum.)

A SNOWY SCENE IN CANASTOTA—WAGON TRACKS ALONG PETERBORO STREET LOOKING SOUTH. (Canastota Canal Town Corporation.)

PETERBORO STREET IN CANASTOTA (POSTCARD), BEFORE THE MODERN ERA OF PAVED STREETS AND HIGH-POWERED HORSELESS CARRIAGES. (Canastota Canal Town Museum.)

SOUTH PETERBORO STREET IN 1905 (POSTCARD), JUST SOUTH OF THE LIFT BRIDGE OVER THE CANAL. The once-famous Bruce Opera House is on the left (arrow). (Canastota Canal Town Museum.)

PETERBORO STREET, C. 1937 (POSTCARD). (Canastota Canal Town Museum.)

RESIDENCES ALONG PETERBORO STREET (POSTCARD). (Canastota Canal Town Museum.)

A MODERN POSTCARD. It shows the Canastota Canal Town Museum, located at 122 N. Canal Street, along the historic Erie Canal. The building dates from the mid-1800s and houses authentic canal-era memorabilia and exhibits. (Author's collection.)

AN EARLY POSTCARD VIEW OF PROSPECT STREET, CANASTOTA. (Canastota Canal Town Museum.)

THE RESIDENCE OF P.F. MILMOE (POSTCARD). The Milmoe family owned and ran the town newspaper, the *Canastota Bee-Journal*, for over 50 years. (Canastota Canal Town Museum.)

AN EARLY 1900S POSTCARD VIEW OF THE MASONIC TEMPLE IN CANASTOTA. (Canastota Canal Town Museum.)

A CLOSE-UP VIEW (POSTCARD) OF THE MASONIC TEMPLE. (Canastota Canal Town Museum.)

A POSTCARD VIEW OF THE MILTON DELANO RESIDENCE, CANASTOTA. DeLano served as clerk of the Town of Lenox, was twice elected sheriff of Madison County, and was a member of Congress, 1888–92. A New York State historic marker has been placed near the building on Peterboro Street. (Canastota Canal Town Museum.)

ANOTHER POSTCARD VIEW OF THE MILTON DELANO RESIDENCE ON PETERBORO STREET, c. 1905. The building is now occupied by the American Legion. (Canastota Canal Town Museum.)

THE F.F. HUBBARD RESIDENCE (POSTCARD, 1911). (Canastota Canal Town Museum.)

THE BURDETTE GUY RESIDENCE ON NORTH MAIN STREET (POSTCARD). (Canastota Canal Town Museum.)

CANASTOTA ACADEMY AT THE TURN OF CENTURY WITH THE SPENCER STREET SCHOOL IN BACKGROUND. Classes were conducted here until 1927. The first school in Canastota was a simple log cabin located at the intersection of Main Street where the Erie Canal was later built. The Canastota school district was formed in 1820. The above buildings were remodeled and added to several times between 1877 and 1927, when a new high school was opened on North Peterboro Street. The earlier schools were then used for kindergarten and elementary grades. In March 1949, a flash fire destroyed the Chapel Street School, and students had to be transferred, some to the local Presbyterian and Methodist churches. The site became a park. (Canastota Canal Town Museum.)

CANASTOTA'S FIRST GIRLS BASKETBALL TEAM,
1910. (Chittenango Village Historian.)

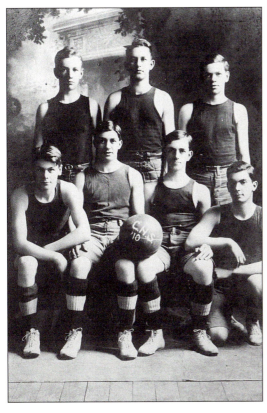

BOYS BASKETBALL, CANASTOTA, 1910.
(Chittenango Village Historian.)

THE ROBERT STREET SCHOOL (POSTCARD). (Canastota Canal Town Museum.)

CANASTOTA POSTCARDS. They depict the life of the village—educational, civic, and political events, complete with flags and banners. (Canastota Canal Town Museum.)

THE EVERGREENS, CANASTOTA (POSTCARD). (Canastota Canal Town Museum.)

THE TERRACE IN CANASTOTA. It overlooked the railroad tracks below (postcard, *c.* 1904). (Canastota Canal Town Museum.)

THE TERRACE—A CLOSE-UP VIEW. (Canastota Canal Town Museum.)

THE TERRACE, CANASTOTA, N. Y.

THE TERRACE, SHOWING THE RAILROAD TRACKS BELOW, 1908. (Canastota Canal Town Museum.)

THE FIRE DEPARTMENT AND CITY HALL AT THE TURN OF THE CENTURY. Up until the installation of a city water system in 1885, Canastota firefighters had to depend upon water from the Erie Canal and Canastota Creek. The building burned in 1916 after over six decades of public service. (Canastota Canal Town Museum.)

Fire Department and City Hall. Canastota, N. Y.

WEST CENTER STREET (POSTCARD). (Chittenango Village Historian.)

THE CANASTOTA CANAL TOWN MUSEUM BUILDING (BEFORE RENOVATION TO MUSEUM). The building, dating from 1860 and located a half-mile south of New York State Thruway Exit 34 on the banks of the original Erie Canal, was dedicated on August 15, 1970. (Canastota Canal Town Museum.)

THE FIRST PRESBYTERIAN CHURCH, CANASTOTA (POSTCARD, 1940S). (Chittenango Village Historian.)

AMELIA EARHART AT THE DEDICATION OF A NEW AIRFIELD. In 1927, the Canastota Village Board voted to appropriate $45,000 under a bond issue for an airport. The village acquired some 209 acres of land from the Goodhand Clark farm, Wm. J. Taylor farm, and Huffman farm. The dedication ceremony for the new airfield, considered the best in the state at the time, was held August 28, 1928, and Mayor Dr. H.G. Gerner declared it a village holiday. Lady Lindy—Miss Earhart—was on hand to dedicate the field. (*Official Commemorative Book*—1985.)

THE NEW AIRPORT. It was a busy place. (*Official Commemorative Book*—1985.)

ROUTE 5 AT MAIN STREET, CANASTOTA, IN THE 1930S. (Canastota Canal Town Museum.)

THE THRUWAY DEDICATION. The New York State Thruway was officially opened for a 115-mile stretch on June 24, 1954. Ribbon-cutting ceremonies were held at every interchange along the opened section. In Canastota, over 3,500 persons were on hand to greet Gov. Thomas E. Dewey and a cavalcade of cars arriving about 10:30 a.m. for the ceremonies. Canastota's State Sen. Wheeler Milmoe was general chairman for the village event. (Canastota Canal Town Museum.)

Three

THE BUSINESS LIFE
OF THE VILLAGE

Canastota was settled in the early 1800s and grew quickly as the Seneca Pike and, later, the new Erie Canal brought jobs and people into the area. The section of the canal through Canastota, with its canal basin (or wide water), was completed in 1820, just ten years after the founding of the village by Reuben Perkins. The developing economy benefited also from agriculture, notably onions and celery, grown in the nearby mucklands. In addition, prominent businesses got their start there or were relocated to Canastota, whose diverse factories brought wide recognition for boats and launches, bobsleds and coaster wagons, early film equipment, and other products. The Biograph, associated with the first moving pictures or "movies," was developed by a local firm and had its first public viewing in Canastota.

The village also saw the growth of other industries: coal and lumber, gasoline engines, a rake factory, and the famous world-renown Watson dumping wagons. After the turn of the century, the Ideal Cut Glass Company produced its prestigious Diamond Poinsettia and Biltmore patterns in its Canastota plant, for 28 years turning out these and others favored by homemakers of the times for vases, bowls, candy dishes, and other kinds of glassware.

FARMING. This postcard hailed one of Canastota's thriving industries—farming, especially onions and celery. At one time Canastota produced more onions than any other area in the world. It was called "Oniontown." (Canastota Canal Town Museum.)

LAUNCHES AND BARGES. They are tied up near the Canastota Celery Co. building in this scene looking east along the canal. (Laws collection, Chittenango Landing Canal Boat Museum.)

CANASTOTA CELERY FIELDS, C. 1909 (POSTCARD). (Chittenango Village Historian.)

A FIELD OF ONIONS, c. 1915. In the 1920s and 1930s, Canastota was considered the onion capital of the United States. (*Official Commemorative Book—1985.*)

THE CANASTOTA BEE (LATER THE BEE-JOURNAL). It was established in 1865, and was owned and operated by the Milmoe family after 1887. The *Journal,* founded in 1881, was consolidated with the *Bee* in 1921. Wheeler Milmoe, republican assemblyman and state senator for many years, served for 50 years (1918–68) as publisher of the newspaper. (Canastota Canal Town Museum.)

A VIEW OF NEW CANAL WALL AND BRIDGE WORK AT THE MAIN STREET CROSSING. Behind the bridge abutment can be seen one of the first hotels on Canal Street along the Erie. It was owned and operated by James E. Conley. The building at the right, Joe's Seafood Market when the picture was taken, is believed to have been constructed in the 1850s. (Canastota Canal Town Museum.)

WALL CONSTRUCTION ON THE CANAL ALONG DEW'S COAL AND LUMBERYARD. At the extreme left is the feed mill; next to it is a canal grocery, which was torn down in 1970. (Canastota Canal Town Museum.)

THE **D.M. TUTTLE CO.** This manufacturer of gasoline engines and launches plied its trade along the famous waterway in Canastota. (Canastota Canal Town Museum.)

THE **CANASTOTA RAKE FACTORY.** It suffered a disastrous fire in the fall of 1907. (Laws collection, Chittenango Landing Canal Boat Museum.)

THE RUINS OF THE RAKE FACTORY. They smoldered as firefighters vainly put hoses to work, October 22, 1907. (Laws collection, Chittenango Landing Canal Boat Museum.)

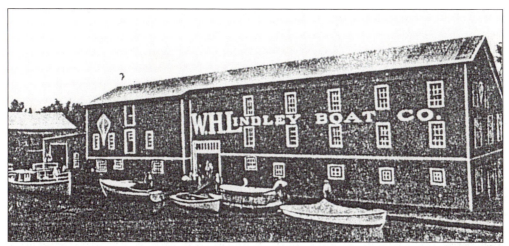

CANASTOTA'S LINDLEY BOATS. Designed by practical boat builders for boat lovers, the Lindley boats, the company boasted, were found from the Florida keys to Canada. (Lindley brochure; Canastota Canal Town Museum.)

CANASTOTA HERALD

POWER PRESS

PRINTING   ESTABLISHMENT.

JOHN GREENHOW. & SON, Publishers,

Canastota, Madison Co., N. Y.

A weekly paper, devoted to Politics, Literature, Local and General News, &c., &c. One of the most extensively circulated periodicals in Madison County. Advertisements inserted at low rates. All kinds of

BOOK & JOB PRINTING

DONE WITH NEATNESS AND DISPATCH.

AN ADVERTISEMENT IN THE *MADISON COUNTY BUSINESS DIRECTORY*, 1860S. (Canastota Canal Town Museum.)

THE FAMOUS WATSON WAGON CO. (POSTCARD). In 1886, Daniel Watson built his first successful dumping wagon in Stratford and moved his plant to Canastota in 1893. The Watson Wagon became world renown, and the company expanded dramatically after the turn of the century. Watson retired in 1908, and his holdings were purchased by Levi Chapman and A.A. Kessler, who continued to expand the wagon business. In World War I, thousands of the sturdy wagons were used in France and elsewhere. In later years, the plant manufactured tractor and school bus bodies. Mechanized wartime equipment was produced at the site during World War II. (Canastota Canal Town Museum.)

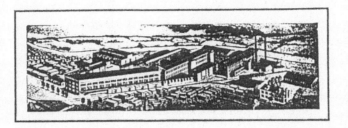

¶ The Watson Factory every year
turns out more dump wagons
than any other factory in the world.
Any Watson user can tell you why.

A PAGE FROM AN EARLY WATSON ADVERTISING BOOKLET. It included a picture of the factory along with the company's claims for its products. (Canastota Canal Town Museum.)

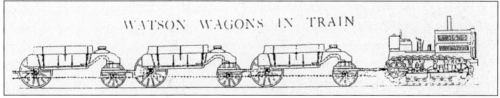

WATSON WAGONS IN TRAIN BEHIND A TRACTOR. This mode of transportation provided the most economical way to move material, when there was any considerable amount to be moved. According to the company, they provided the "lowest initial cost of any given hauling capacity" and, it was said, "They depreciate much slower than motor truck equipment." (Canastota Canal Town Museum.)

THE SHERWOOD BROS. MANUFACTURING CO. The company, pioneers in coaster wagons and steerable sleds, advertised that they catered to boys of all ages. Their spring coaster wagon was equipped with shock absorbers, and their sleds were made for speed and steering efficiency. (Canastota Canal Town Museum.)

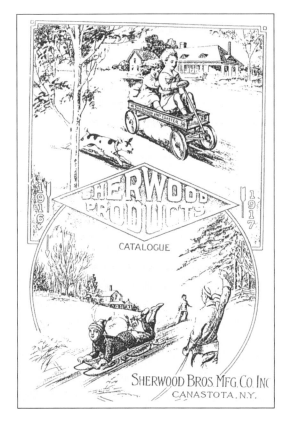

THE COVER OF THE 1917 SHERWOOD PRODUCTS CATALOGUE. It shows children enjoying a ride in a "Sherwood Coaster" wagon and a youngster with a Sherwood sled on a winter hill. (Canastota Canal Town Museum.)

THE COVER PHOTOGRAPH OF AN IDEAL CUT GLASS COMPANY SALES BOOKLET, C. 1918. The company was founded in 1903 in Corning, New York, by Luman Conover, Fred Johnson, and Charles Rose. Both Rose and Johnson were experienced glasscutters; Conover was a financier. A Syracuse distributor, the W.P. Hitchcock Company, contracted for the firm's entire production. Hitchcock purchased Ideal in 1905 and, having once owned a jewelry store in Canastota, relocated the glass company to the village. It was moved into an unoccupied factory building and offices on East Canal Street formerly used by the Marvin Drill Co. Charles Rose became factory superintendent of the Canastota plant.

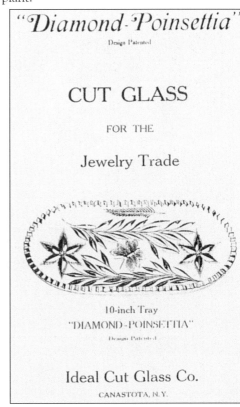

THE STAR FLOWER PATTERN (MORE COMMONLY KNOWN AS "DIAMOND POINSETTIA"). The design was patented in 1913. It was Ideal's most expensive. It was also the most popular and most collected. (Canastota Canal Town Museum.)

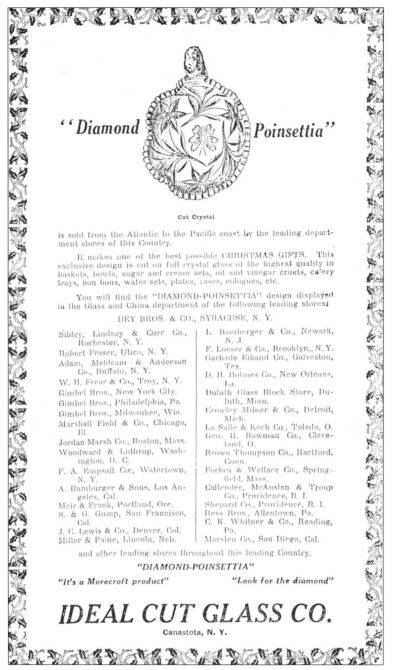

"Diamond Poinsettia"

Cut Crystal

is sold from the Atlantic to the Pacific coast by the leading department stores of this Country.

It makes one of the best possible CHRISTMAS GIFTS. This exclusive design is cut on full crystal glass of the highest quality in baskets, bowls, sugar and cream sets, oil and vinegar cruets, celery trays, bon bons, water sets, plates, vases, colognes, etc.

You will find the "DIAMOND-POINSETTIA" design displayed in the Glass and China department of the following leading stores:

DEY BROS. & CO., SYRACUSE, N. Y.

Sibley, Lindsay & Curr Co., Rochester, N. Y.
Robert Fraser, Utica, N. Y.
Adam, Meldram & Anderson Co., Buffalo, N. Y.
W. H. Frear & Co., Troy, N. Y.
Gimbel Bros., New York City.
Gimbel Bros., Philadelphia, Pa.
Gimbel Bros., Milwaukee, Wis.
Marshall Field & Co., Chicago, Ill.
Jordan Marsh Co., Boston, Mass.
Woodward & Lothrop, Washington, D. C.
F. A. Empsall Co., Watertown, N. Y.
A. Hamburger & Sons, Los Angeles, Cal.
Meir & Frank, Portland, Ore.
S. & G. Gump, San Francisco, Cal.
J. C. Lewis & Co., Denver, Col.
Miller & Paine, Lincoln, Neb.

L. Bamberger & Co., Newark, N. J.
F. Loeser & Co., Brooklyn,, N. Y.
Garbade Eiband Co., Galveston, Tex.
D. H. Holmes Co., New Orleans, La.
Duluth Glass Block Store, Duluth, Minn.
Crowley Milner & Co., Detroit, Mich.
La Salle & Koch Co., Toledo, O.
Geo. H. Bowman Co., Cleveland, O.
Brown Thompson Co., Hartford, Conn.
Forbes & Wallace Co., Springfield, Mass.
Callender, McAuslan & Troup Co., Providence, R. I.
Shepard Co., Providence, R. I.
Hess Bros., Allentown, Pa.
C. K. Whitner & Co., Reading, Pa.
Marston Co., San Diego, Cal.

and other leading stores throughout this leading Country.

"DIAMOND-POINSETTIA"

"It's a Morecroft product"   "Look for the diamond"

IDEAL CUT GLASS CO.
Canastota, N. Y.

AN ADVERTISEMENT FOR THE "DIAMOND POINSETTIA" (C. 1918). The company said they distributed "from the Atlantic to the Pacific coast" and listed some of the stores selling this and other Ideal Cut Glass Co. patterns, including such well-known upstate New York department stores as Sibley (Rochester), Dey Bros. and Adam, Meldram & Anderson (Syracuse), and W.H. Frear (Troy), as well as national names like Marshall Field (Chicago), Gimbel (New York), Woodward & Lothrop (Washington, D.C.), Forbes & Wallace (Springfield), the Shepard Co. (Providence), and Jordan Marsh (Boston). (Canastota Canal Town Museum.)

68

No 3. FLORAL. Celery. $7.50

No 3. FLORAL. Spooner. $5.00

IDEAL'S FLORAL PATTERN. (Ideal Cut Glass Company Plate 65, courtesy Canastota Canal Town Museum.)

EXCELSOR.
No. 830. 1 Quart Water Bottle, $7.00 each.

VASES IN THE IDEAL CUT GLASS COMPANY LINE. (Ideal Cut Glass Company Plate 15, courtesy Canastota Canal Town Museum.)

CUT GLASS COMPANY EMPLOYEES, 1912. (Canastota Canal Town Museum.)

FARR BROS. HARDWARE. Opened in 1880, it was hailed as "the oldest store in the village" by the writers of the *Official Commemorative Book* for Canastota's 175th birthday celebration in 1985. This extremely old, mounted sepia-tone photograph is in the collection of the Canastota Canal Town Museum.

THE PETERBORO STREET BRIDGE UNDER CONSTRUCTION, 1899. (Canastota Canal Town Museum.)

CENTER STREET, C. 1900. This was one of the busy streets in early Canastota. (Canastota Canal Town Museum.)

PETERBORO STREET IN THE 1920S. In the middle of the block in this scene, on the east side of Peterboro Street, is the State Bank. (Canastota Canal Town Museum.)

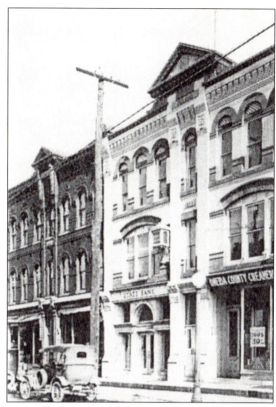

THE REMODELED STATE BANK BUILDING IN CANASTOTA, NOT FAR FROM THE OLD CANAL. (Canastota Canal Town Museum.)

STREET VIEWS ON A TRIPLE MAILING CARD. Back in the days of the 1¢ postage stamp, tourists and townsfolk alike got an added bargain with this triple-size mailing card showing Canastota streets. For a 1¢ stamp, one could mail the card folded or rolled. The address side cautions,

THE FARR BROS. HARDWARE STORE JUST BEFORE ITS CLOSING IN THE 1980s. (*Official Commemorative Book—1985.*)

however, that the card could be mailed for "One Cent without Writing, Two Cents with Writing." A number of older establishments can be seen on the streets in this unusual panoramic postcard. (Canastota Canal Town Museum.)

THE WHITE ELEPHANT, A VILLAGE FAVORITE AT 112 CENTER STREET. It was called "central New York's finest restaurant" in Canastota's *Official Commemorative Book—1985*.

THE PETERBORO STREET BUSINESS SECTION IN THE 1940S (POSTCARD). (Canastota Canal Town Museum.)

A LATER POSTCARD VIEW OF THE BUSINESS DISTRICT ALONG PETERBORO STREET. Above the drugstore entrance, the elephant logo sign hangs as a reminder of the former White Elephant restaurant, popular for many years, just around the corner on Center Street. (Canastota Canal Town Museum.)

Four
HOLLYWOOD AND GLITTER

Both villages have, in a sense, "gone Hollywood." The pictures in this chapter reflect the area's connection with American film and the related literature.

For Chittenango, the story of a Kansas lass named Dorothy and her little dog Toto walking the famous Yellow Brick Road to the Emerald City of Oz has become an American legend. That story, which became the MGM film *The Wizard of Oz,* was the creation of Chittenango-born author L. Frank Baum. Each spring since the early 1980s, the village celebrates Dorothy and Toto, the Scarecrow, the Tin Woodman, the Cowardly Lion, and the delightful little Munchkins with a parade and festive goings-on.

For Canastota, the village provided the setting in part for actor Henry Fonda's film role as Chad Hanna, a Canastota youth who joined up with a traveling circus in the upstate New York of the 1830s. The novel by Walter D. Edmonds, which appeared originally as *Red Wheels Rolling* in *The Saturday Evening Post,* was published in book form as *Chad Hanna* (1940) and quickly went to Hollywood. Edmonds's third novel to become a major motion picture, the movie was also the third to star Henry Fonda, himself tied to a family of upstate New York settlers who gave their name to the town of Fonda, further east along the canal on the Mohawk River.

It is appropriate that Canastota and Chittenango be represented in the film industry, for the pioneer motion picture process, the "Biograph," was developed and premiered here.

THE FRONT END PAPERS OF WALTER D. EDMONDS'S NOVEL *CHAD HANNA* (1940). It depicts the Yellow Bud Tavern on the Erie Canal at Canastota. Set in the 1830s, the novel tells the story of a Canastota lad who joins a traveling circus troupe. The book was the third Edmonds novel to become a motion picture with Henry Fonda in the leading role. (Author's collection.)

A LOBBY CARD FOR THE 20TH CENTURY FOX FILM *CHAD HANNA* (1940). The movie was based on the novel by Walter D. Edmonds set in Canastota and upstate New York in the 1830s. (Author's collection.)

A SCENE FROM THE DARRY F. ZANUCK PRODUCTION OF CHAD HANNA. Two rival circuses battle it out. The novel and motion picture featured Canastotans like Chad, the title figure, and local entrepreneur Elias Proops. The picture starred Henry Fonda, Dorothy Lamour, and Linda Darnell, and also featured Guy Kibbe, Jane Darwell, and John Carradine. (Author's collection.)

A CANAL SCENE IN THE CHITTENANGO-CANASTOTA-ROME AREA. This scene is from another film based on an Edmonds novel. In all, Henry Fonda starred in three of these films—as a young canal boat captain in the Hollywood version of *Rome Haul* (above), as the Canastota youth who joined the circus in *Chad Hanna*, and as the patriot farmer in the epic *Drums Along the Mohawk*. (Author's collection.)

THE PRESS ANNOUNCEMENT FOR THE TELEVISION RE-RELEASE OF THE MOVIE *CHAD HANNA.* It begins in Canastota and deals with a touring circus troupe that drew a Canastota youth into its theatrical fold. (National Telefilm Associates, Inc.)

CHITTENANGO—THE BIRTHPLACE OF L. FRANK BAUM. This Chittenango Foundation sign on State Route 5 greets travelers entering the village from the east. Born on May 15, 1856, Baum was the seventh child of Benjamin and Cynthia Baum. His father's family came to America in 1748 seeking religious freedom, and his grandfather was a Methodist minister who rode the circuit from town to town. His mother's family, of Scotch-Irish descent, came to New York from Connecticut. When Frank was born, his father was a cooper, or maker of barrels, and his Chittenango land included the family homestead, a barrel factory, and a boardinghouse for workers. When oil was discovered nearby he went into the oil business and made a fortune. When Frank was five, the family moved to a 15-acre farm north of Syracuse, in what is now the suburb of Mattydale. (Photograph by the author.)

OZFEST, THE 15TH OZ PARADE, MAY 15, 1993. Each May the Chittenango Foundation's Oz Committee sponsors this festival to celebrate the birth of L. Frank Baum, author of *The Wonderful Wizard of Oz* and many other children's tales. (Courtesy Richard F. Sullivan, Historian, Village of Chittenango.)

JUDY GARLAND AS DOROTHY IN THE MGM MOTION PICTURE *THE WIZARD OF OZ.* The movie was based on a book by L. Frank Baum, who was born in Chittenango. (Author's collection.)

BILLIE BURKE IN *THE WIZARD OF OZ.* Her character befriends Dorothy as she travels to the Emerald City of Oz. (Author's collection.)

THE WICKED WITCH OF THE WEST, ACTRESS MARGARET HAMILTON. She confronts Dorothy (Judy Garland) in a scene from the MGM picture based on L. Frank Baum's *The Wonderful Wizard of Oz.* (Author's collection.)

ALONG THE YELLOW BRICK ROAD. Dorothy (Judy Garland) gets the help of the Scarecrow (Ray Bolger) and the Tin Woodman (Jack Haley), as her little dog, Toto, watches cautiously. (Author's collection.)

ANOTHER VIEW OF THE PARADE IN CHITTENANGO IN MAY 1993. (Courtesy Richard Sullivan.)

THE SCARECROW, TIN WOODMAN, AND COWARDLY LION IN THE 14TH ANNUAL OZ PARADE IN THE VILLAGE, 1992. The Cowardly Lion is talking to children near curbside. (Courtesy Richard Sullivan.)

ANOTHER VIEW OF THE 1992 PARADE. (Courtesy Richard Sullivan.)

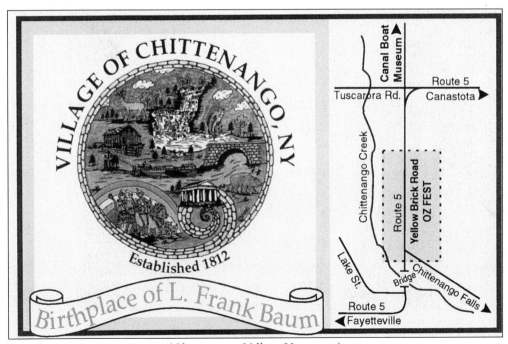

A PARADE ROUTE POSTCARD. (Chittenango Village Historian.)

THE SYRACUSE NEWSPAPERS FLOAT IN THE ANNUAL OZ PARADE IN CHITTENANGO, 1992. It focuses upon the Munchkins, those delightful little people in the L. Frank Baum story. (Courtesy Richard Sullivan.)

THE SULLIVAN FREE LIBRARY FLOAT IN THE 1996 PARADE. (Courtesy Karen Fauls-Traynor, Sullivan Free Library, Chittenango.)

Five

CHITTENANGO:
MERCANTILE AND
COMMERCIAL ACTIVITIES

Chittenango, settled as the 19th century began, was especially favored by its location. The Great Genesee Road and the Chittenango-Cazenovia Plank Road made it an ideal coach stop. That, plus the fact that notable settlers—or those who would become notable—brought business acumen and political savvy to the town, where numerous locally manufactured products began to spread the village name throughout the state.

Having seceded from the Town of Cazenovia in 1803, the Chittenango area became the Town of Sullivan, named for a general with military experience in the region. "Sullivan" can also be found in several institutional and place names like Sullivan Academy and the Sullivan Free Library. On the county level, Chittenango is part of Madison County, formed in 1806.

By 1833 the village had a barrel factory, an iron foundry, and a machine shop, as well as blacksmith and carriage shops, followed by sawmills and a paper mill in the 1850s. As the village grew, plants for manufacturing valves and pottery could be found. On the Erie Canal, a canning factory and general provisions store were located at Chittenango Landing, where dry-dock facilities for boat building and repair added to the area's economic success.

THE OLD FOUNDRY AT CHITTENANGO (POSTCARD). (Chittenango Landing Canal Boat Museum.)

THE CHITTENANGO ROLLER MILLS. This plant operated for a long time in the late 1800s under Ransford Button. It was sold to E.H. Cook in 1904. (Chittenango Village Historian.)

LISTINGS IN THE *MADISON COUNTY BUSINESS DIRECTORY* IN THE 1860S. They included advertising for Dixon's Hotel and Ransford Button's Chittenango Mills. (Canastota Canal Town Museum.)

Dixon's Hotel,

Chittenango, N. Y.

SAMUEL C. DIXON, Prop.

A comfortable house, conveniently located.   The proprietor will spare no efforts to render the visits of guests pleasant and agreeable.

Good Stabling Attached.

RANSFORD BUTTON,

MERCHANT MILLER,

Proprietor of the CHITTENANGO MILLS,

CHITTENANGO,   N. Y.

Manufacturer of Superior Grades of Flour, Feed, &c. ☞ Cash paid for Grain.

OLD BLACKSMITH AND CARRIAGE SHOPS. (Chittenango Landing Canal Boat Museum.)

91

THE CRIST VALVE MANUFACTURING CO., CHITTENANGO. The building dates from 1820. (Chittenango Landing Canal Boat Museum.)

A POSTCARD SHOWING CRIST VALVE. According to the correspondent, the plant was not running at the time this postcard was mailed (December 1908). (Chittenango Village Historian.)

CHITTENANGO POTTERY. Another of the old Chittenango factories, this one was located along the original canal. (Courtesy Dr. Robert E. Hager, Chittenango Landing Canal Boat Museum.)

CHITTENANGO POTTERY (POSTCARD). Another view of the pottery plant, this is the side facing away from the canal. (Chittenango Village Historian.)

FRANKLIN HOSLEY AND HIS WIFE, HELEN. Hosley was the proprietor of the Chittenango Landing Dry Dock, Store, & Warehouse in 1878. (Courtesy of Barbara H. Richardson and Chittenango Landing Canal Boat Museum.)

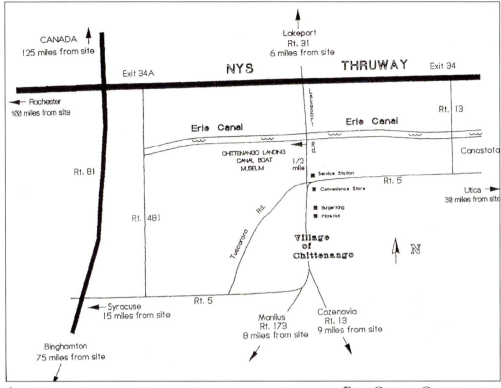

A MAP SHOWING THE RELATIVE POSITION OF THE ORIGINAL ERIE CANAL, CHITTENANGO LANDING (NOW A STATE AND NATIONAL HISTORIC SITE), AND THE VILLAGE OF CHITTENANGO. (Chittenango Landing Canal Boat Museum.)

PART OF DRY-DOCK BAY AT THE ORIGINAL CHITTENANGO LANDING ON THE ERIE CANAL. Today, the restored site is part of the Chittenango Landing Canal Boat Museum. (Photograph permission of the Museum.)

A WEST VIEW OF THE MERRILL-SOULE COMPANY CANNING FACTORY, 1909, SITUATED ON THE CANAL. (Chittenango Village Historian.)

ANOTHER VIEW OF THE CANNING FACTORY AND DRY DOCK. Besides this Chittenango company, several other Madison County businesses handled the locally grown corn, beets, and peas, including the Burt Olney Canning Co. in Oneida, the Leonardsville Canning Co., and the Oldney & Ford and Tuft's canning factories of Canastota. (Chittenango Landing Canal Boat Museum.)

THE CANNING FACTORY, CHITTENANGO LANDING. After the turn of the century, canal boats were using the new and enlarged Barge Canal that ran further to the north, but some old sections of the original canal were still in use, including the adjacent dry dock area (far right). As the sign painted on the building shows, the canning factory was the manufacturer of None-Such Mincemeat, a holiday favorite for mincemeat pie still much in vogue. (Courtesy Dr. Robert E. Hager, Chittenango Landing Canal Boat Museum.)

WORKING THE "BIG DITCH." This is another view of the *Satie Hughes* (see chapter one) out of Fort Hunter. (Chittenango Landing Canal Boat Museum.)

"Lumber Boats at Chittenango." Along the Erie Canal at Chittenango soon after sunrise on a June morning, c. 1907, a span of horse-drawn lumber boats plods slowly past the Merrill-Soule Cannery on their way from Tonawanda toward Albany. The painting by Robert E. Hager, D.D.S., was done in oil on masonite. (Photograph by the artist; used with permission.)

CANAL BOAT WORKERS AT CHITTENANGO LANDING. (From *Chittenango Landing, The Past Revisited*, 1993, Chittenango Landing Canal Boat Museum.)

JOHN CRYAN'S BLACKSMITH SHOP IN CHITTENANGO, C. 1910–12. (Chittenango Landing Canal Boat Museum.)

SENECA STREET, CHITTENANGO, 1924. This postcard view of downtown Chittenango shows some of the businesses of the period. (Chittenango Landing Canal Boat Museum.)

THE SHEFFORD CHEESE CO., INC. Employees of the cheese company stand in front of the factory in a 1925 photograph. The company manufactured Shefford Snappy Cheese. The site later was occupied by the Cazenovia Equipment Co. (Chittenango Landing Canal Boat Museum.)

"CHITTENANGO CLEARS STREETS MODERN WAY." That is how a local newspaper put it on February 9, 1940. Snow and ice were removed from New York State Route 5 in the business section of the village with a tractor and grading equipment used by E.J. Button & Sons in grading the Johnson curve cut-off east of the village the year before. The town first broke up the packed snow and ice; then, a tractor pulled the hydraulic-operated grader over the road, and the snow and ice were pealed from the concrete and loaded for carting away. The work was done by town equipment and E.J. Button & Sons, under direction of village officers. "It was a good job, too," said the reporter. (Chittenango Landing Canal Boat Museum.)

PATTINSON CHEVROLET, 1945. A longtime car dealership in the village, the Pattinson site was later Sun Chevrolet. (Chittenango Landing Canal Boat Museum.)

RAMBLERS SOLD HERE. In the 1950s, this auto dealership was located in the Newtown building. (Chittenango Landing Canal Boat Museum.)

THE ORIGINAL HAM THAT AM HAM RESTAURANT. Over 50 years in business at this Route 5 location when this postcard was issued, the restaurant menu, it said, featured "real COUNTRY SMOKED HAMS from our own smoke house. Tender and flavorful." It also noted that "Mail orders for hams accepted." (Chittenango Village Historian.)

Six

VIEWS IN AND
AROUND CHITTENANGO

The village boasted early the benefits of culture—an opera house, a library, an academy, and also a bank and post office, as well as the offices and shops of area entrepreneurs.

Just outside the village to the north, Chittenango Station grew with the railroad fever of the times, serving the New York Central Rail Road, the Hudson River Rail Road, and other lines. To the southwest, on the Cazenovia Road, the popular Chittenango Falls featured a cascading waterfall as high as Niagara that drew countless visitors, especially during the summer months, and, during much of the 1800s, Chittenango White Sulphur Springs offered tourists from all over an inviting resort complex of hotel and cottages. In the 1880s, a renovated White Sulphur Springs advertised its convenience just "four miles South of Chittenango Station on N.Y. Central R.R." as a health institution and watering place celebrated for its medical waters and providing hot baths, boating, fishing, bowling, billiards, and croquet. Both the falls and the springs were on Chittenango Creek, crossing the Seneca Pike at the western edge of the village on its way north.

Today, the Chittenango Landing Canal Boat Museum, located off Lakeport Road on the original Erie, is an historic preservation site and an active archeological project. A three-bay dry dock where canal boats were built and repaired in the 19th and early 20th centuries has been excavated and fitted with reconstructed mitre and drop gates. An on-site interpretive center and library provide hands-on activities and exhibits. A picnic area and related sawmill and blacksmith shop are also on the premises. At Chittenango Falls today, the State Park Service offers places to fish, hike, and picnic. The annual OzFest (see chapter four) honors the birth of L. Frank Baum, author of *The Wonderful Wizard of Oz* and many other stories.

CHITTENANGO CREEK, SOUTH OF THE VILLAGE, ABOUT 1906. The postcard pictures the valley in the vicinity of the Baum barrel factory. (Chittenango Village Historian.)

CHITTENANGO CREEK. The postcard scene is from a photograph made by Charles P. Marshall in 1897. (Chittenango Village Historian.)

A FLYER ADVERTISING CHITTENANGO WHITE SULPHUR SPRINGS, ON CHITTENANGO CREEK, A POPULAR SUMMER RESORT IN THE 1800S. In the heyday of the sulphur spas in upstate New York, summer vacationers from the often humid and oppressive large eastern cities like Boston and New York sought out the country atmosphere of the spas at Chittenango and others at Saratoga, Ballston, and Richfield Springs. (Chittenango Landing Canal Boat Museum.)

Chittenango White Sulphur Springs, Chittenango, N. Y.   Published by Geo. C. Clark.

CHITTENANGO WHITE SULPHUR SPRINGS. This postcard (1893?) pictures the hotel on the east side of the creek, and cottages on the west side. (Chittenango Village Historian.)

CHITTENANGO SPRINGS, 1897. The springs can be seen in the background on the hillside between the buildings. (Chittenango Village Historian.)

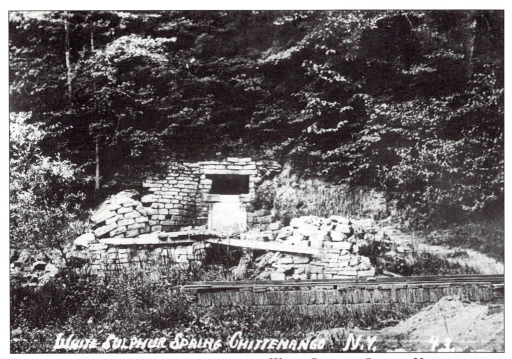

A CLOSE-UP OF THE SPRING AT THE SITE OF THE WHITE SULPHUR SPRINGS HOTEL COMPLEX. The hotel was gone by 1905, but the spring remains along the road to Cazenovia. (Chittenango Village Historian.)

SIG SAUTELL'S CIRCUS AT THE WHITE SULPHUR SPRINGS HOTEL. The Sautell Circus was a popular attraction in the area, and in other villages and towns along the canal route. It traveled the canal and sometimes wintered in nearby Syracuse. (Canastota Canal Town Museum.)

CHITTENANGO FALLS IN THE OLD DAYS. Visitors came in horse-drawn buggies to appreciate the beauty of the falls. (Chittenango Landing Canal Boat Museum.)

CHITTENANGO FALLS (POSTCARD), C. 1910. (Chittenango Village Historian.)

CHITTENANGO FALLS, 1985. This photograph shows the falls before the coming season changes the site into the lush green foliage of summer. (New York State Office of Parks, Recreation, and Historic Preservation, Central Region.)

CHITTENANGO FALLS IN SUMMER. (New York State Office of Parks, Recreation, and Historic Preservation, Central Region.)

STAIRS TO TOP OF FALLS, CHITTENANGO FALLS STATE PARK, SEPTEMBER 1979. (New York State Office of Parks, Recreation, and Historic Preservation, Central Region.)

A FISHING SPOT, CHITTENANGO CREEK, SEPTEMBER 1988. The creek runs north through the village of Chittenango. (New York State Office of Parks, Recreation, and Historic Preservation, Central Region.)

WALRATH BRIDGE. Built in 1884 by the foundry owner, the bridge crossed Chittenango Creek on what is now Genesee Street (Route 5). (Chittenango Landing Canal Boat Museum.)

CHITTENANGO CREEK, ABOUT 1910. The bridge over Route 5 can be seen in the distance. (Chittenango Village Historian.)

A VIEW OF MAIN STREET, CHITTENANGO, 1911. (Chittenango Landing Canal Boat Museum.)

GATES FOUNTAIN AND PARK, 1910. This postcard shows the drinking fountains, one for the public and another for horses. (Chittenango Village Historian.)

AN EARLY 1900S VIEW OF CHITTENANGO'S MAIN STREET. It looks toward the business district of the village. (Chittenango Landing Canal Boat Museum.)

ANOTHER VIEW OF MAIN STREET IN THE EARLY AUTOMOBILE DAYS. (Chittenango Village Historian.)

AN EARLY 1930S STREET SCENE SHOWING THE LOCAL THEATER, THE DELPHIA, A SHOE STORE, AND THE FIREHOUSE. (Chittenango Village Historian.)

CARL'S OPERA HOUSE. Standing prominently on Genesee Street, the opera house was part of the cultural hub of the village. (Chittenango Landing Canal Boat Museum.)

YATES HIGH SCHOOL, 1909. The Yates High School included the old Yates Academy. (Chittenango Landing Canal Boat Museum.)

YATES HIGH SCHOOL (POSTCARD, C. 1906). The building was torn down in 1930. (Courtesy Barbara H. Richardson.)

YATES SCHOOL PUPILS (POSTCARD). (Chittenango Village Historian.)

ANOTHER YATES HIGH SCHOOL POSTCARD, C. 1910. (Chittenango Village Historian.)

A STREET SCENE IN CHITTENANGO, 1923 (POSTCARD). (Chittenango Village Historian.)

POLYTECHNIC STREET IN THE 1920S (POSTCARD). (Chittenango Village Historian.)

A POSTCARD SHOWING "THE NORMANDIE." It was billed as "a unique home for discriminating tourists on Route 5." (Chittenango Village Historian.)

THE CHITTENANGO POST OFFICE, 1914. This view shows the village post office in the early 1900s. Later, the building was home to the State Bank of Chittenango. (Chittenango Landing Canal Boat Museum.)

THE POST OFFICE AND GENERAL STORE AT CHITTENANGO STATION. (Chittenango Village Historian.)

THE NEW YORK CENTRAL RAILROAD STATION AT CHITTENANGO STATION, C. 1913. (Chittenango Village Historian.)

RAILROADS AND ROSES.
N. Y. C. AND H. R. R. R.
CHITTENANGO. STATION. N. Y.

ANOTHER EARLY 1900S POSTCARD SHOWING THE ROSE GARDEN AT THE NEW YORK CENTRAL AND HUDSON RIVER RAILROAD STATION AT CHITTENANGO STATION. (Chittenango Village Historian.)

A SCHOOL AT CHITTENANGO STATION, C. 1912–13. (Chittenango Village Historian.)

THE PETERS STORE AT CHITTENANGO STATION (POSTCARD). (Chittenango Village Historian.)

A SKETCH OF THE SULLIVAN FREE LIBRARY IN CHITTENANGO. A library association was organized in November 1947 and received a five-year provisional charter from the Board of Regents the next year. The first librarian was Mrs. Clara Houck, one of the original trustees. Starting out in the fire department building, the library moved in 1963 to a house on McDonnell Street, which was remodeled and then enlarged. In 1977 it temporarily moved to the Tyler Building on Genesee Street, while the McDonnell Street building was razed, and work on a new facility began. The present structure (above) was designed by Syracuse architect Edward Jenner. (Courtesy Karen Fauls-Traynor, Sullivan Free Library, Chittenango.)

Seven

THE BOXING
HALL OF FAME

The International Boxing Hall of Fame, established in 1984 and located at One Hall of Fame Drive in Canastota, just off New York State Thruway (Interstate 95) Exit 34, chronicles a century of boxing history. The Hall of Fame is an outgrowth of a Boxing Showcase honoring the careers of two of Canastota's native sons, boxing champions Carmen Basilio and Billy Backus.

Each year in June, an Induction Weekend, with its Banquet of Champions and other attractions, offers boxing fans and other interested tourists an opportunity to meet boxing legends. The Hall of Fame museum provides displays of photographs of boxers and boxing, and showcases historic memorabilia of the sport, including gloves, robes, ticket stubs, and videotapes related to boxing history. The Hall of Fame is open year-round (except Easter, Thanksgiving, and Christmas holidays).

CANASTOTA-BORN CARMEN BASILIO. In the early 1800s, boxing bouts were staged in Canastota and nearby communities featuring the brawny builders of the Erie Canal, which opened in 1825, and boaters also brought news of bare-knuckle bouts along the canal. The village was the scene of the first showing of a motion picture. Appropriately enough, the film featured a sparring match. High schools in the area included boxing as a major sport into the 1940s. Basilio took both the Welterweight and Middleweight world championships in the 1950s, and his nephew, Billy Backus, was crowned World Welterweight Champion in the 1970s. (Photograph courtesy of International Boxing Hall of Fame.)

BOXING SHOWCASE. The Carmen Basilio-Billy Backus Boxing Showcase was made possible by over $300,000 in donations from local businesses, and salutes the community's involvement in the sport of boxing, particularly the careers of Basilio and Backus. Dedicated August 18, 1984, the showcase contains robes from the fighters, posters, photographs, gloves, and news clips. It was located directly across the street from the planned Boxing Hall of Fame. (Darcy Associates, Ltd.)

THE INTERNATIONAL BOXING HALL OF FAME. An outgrowth of the Carmen Basilio-Billy Backus Showcase, the Hall of Fame was organized as a place to display boxing memorabilia and honor boxing greats, similar to the halls of fame for other sports. The first induction weekend was held June 8–10, 1990, when 46 boxers were chosen by a panel of over one hundred sports writers and historians to become the first members of the Hall of Fame. In addition, seven men who contributed outside the ring to boxing's growth were also honored. Since then, new members of the Hall of Fame are inducted at ceremonies each spring. (Darcy Associates, Ltd.)

A VICTORY TESTIMONIAL DINNER FOR BASILIO. Carmen Basilio's first crown in the 147-pound division came on September 9, 1956, when he dethroned Tony Demarco. He won the 160-pound crown from Ray Robinson a year later. In the photograph above are former heavyweight champion Jimmy Braddock (far left), Ross Patane, Sam Fudesco (co-chairmen of the event), and Basilio. (*Official Commemorative Book—1985.*)

HANDSHAKES FOR CARMEN BASILIO AS HE HEADS OUT OF CANASTOTA FOR A MATCH. (*Official Commemorative Book—1985.*)

ARCHIE MOORE AT CANASTOTA. The legendary boxer appears at the Hall of Fame Museum. (Photograph by Pat Orr, courtesy of International Boxing Hall of Fame.)

**BILLY BACKUS, NEPHEW OF WORLD
CHAMPION CARMEN BASILIO.** Billy was
another Canastota youth who grew up
involved in the sport of boxing. Both
Backus and Basilio were early inductees in
the Boxing Hall of Fame. (Photograph
courtesy of International Boxing Hall of
Fame.)

**THE CNY BOXING APPRECIATION
AWARD.** Tony Graziano of Canastota, long
affiliated with the sport of boxing and
owner of the restaurant Casa Mia on North
Peterboro Street, was chosen in 1993 to
receive the annual Central New York
Boxing Appreciation Award. The award is
presented each year to a person who has
made a significant contribution to boxing
in the area. Graziano was born in Utica,
New York, served in World War II as a
paratrooper, had a brief career as a boxer,
and became a promoter and manager of the
sport. The Hall of Fame press release for the
award event called him a man "truly in love
with the boxing game." (Photograph
courtesy of International Boxing Hall of
Fame.)

ACKNOWLEDGEMENTS

It is a pleasure to acknowledge the cooperation, help, courtesy, and encouragement of personnel at area museums, libraries, and history offices. The book owes much to Dr. Robert E. Hager, a longtime friend, Erie enthusiast, model canal boat builder, and former president of the Chittenango Landing Canal Boat Museum, who photographed countless pictures and postcards from museum holdings and provided information on the history of Chittenango Landing and the restoration work going on. Others at the museum, especially Barbara H. Richardson and Joan DiCristina, are also due thanks. The assistance of Rose Raffa, Canastota Canal Town Museum, was major, covering the loan of many pictures, postcards, and local publications. Richard Sullivan, Chittenango Village Historian, provided postcards and photographs. Karen Keast, New York State Office of Parks, Recreation, and Historic Preservation, Central Region, provided the slides of Chittenango Falls State Park; Jeff Brophy, International Boxing Hall of Fame, provided photographs and information about the museum; and Rene C. Gabriel, Madison County Tourism, set up appointments with local museums and furnished material that substantially eased the research work for the book. Thanks to my grandson, J. Michael Wyld-Chirico, for his help in increasing my computer literacy, and to the skilled staff at Arcadia, especially Rebecca Heflin and Katie White. For friendly advice on photographic matters, thanks go to Jeffrey Owens and Rita M. Sullivan. To my wife, Norma, who sat through many sessions with local historians and museum staffs as the book progressed, my heartfelt thanks for her patiently enduring the hours spent with me on the road in search for material.

A word about entries. Captions generally give the source of photographs and postcards. In the credits, *Official Commemorative Book—1985* is used in lieu of the full title, *Official Commemorative Book, 175th Birthday Celebration of Canastota, New York, July 15–27, 1985*; the book was used through the courtesy of Rose Raffa. When a date appears with a postcard, it is the mailing date if the card was sent. In instances where cards bore no date or the postmark was indistinct, philatelic evidence (such as the postage stamp, its date of issue, and its period of sale) has been used to approximate the date. On occasion, notations of village or museum staff were taken into account. In all instances, the author is responsible for any errors, whether in dating or description.